D1530353

What Happens at an Aquarium?/ ¿Qué pasa en un acuario?

By Barbara Bakowski

Reading Consultant: Susan Nations, M.Ed.,
author/literacy coach/consultant in literacy development

WEEKLY READER®
PUBLISHING

For a complete list of Where People Work titles,
please visit our web site at **www.garethstevens.com**.
For a free catalog describing Gareth Stevens Publishing's list of high-quality books,
call 1-800-542-2595 (USA) or 1-800-387-3178 (Canada). Our fax: 877-542-2596

Library of Congress Cataloging-in-Publication Data

Bakowski, Barbara.
     What happens at an aquarium? / by Barbara Bakowski /
     ¿Qué pasa en un acuario? / por Barbara Bakowski.
        p. cm. — (Where people work)
     Includes bibliographical references and index.
     ISBN-10: 1-4339-0082-3   ISBN-13: 978-1-4339-0082-2 (lib. bdg.)
     ISBN-10: 1-4339-0146-3   ISBN-13: 978-1-4339-0146-1 (softcover)
     1. Aquariums—Juvenile literature. I. Title. II. Title: Qué pasa en un acuario?
  SF457.3.B36   2009b
  639.34'4023—dc22   2008039348

This edition first published in 2009 by
Weekly Reader® Books
An Imprint of Gareth Stevens Publishing
1 Reader's Digest Road
Pleasantville, NY 10570-7000 USA

Executive Managing Editor: Lisa M. Herrington
Creative Director: Lisa Donovan
Designers: Michelle Castro, Alexandria Davis
Photo Researcher: Charlene Pinckney
Publisher: Keith Garton
Translation: Tatiana Acosta and Guillermo Gutiérrez

Photo credits: cover, title page, p. 5 Erik S. Lesser/*The New York Times*/Redux; p. 7 Newscom; p. 9
David Iliff; pp. 11, 13, 15, 19, 21 Courtesy Georgia Aquarium; p. 17 Gene Blythe/AP

The publisher thanks the Georgia Aquarium in Atlanta, Georgia, for their participation in the
development of this book.

Printed in the United States of America

1 2 3 4 5 6 7 8 9 10 09 08

Hi, Kids!

I'm Buddy, your Weekly Reader® pal. Have you ever been to an aquarium? I'm here to show and tell what happens at an aquarium. So, come on. Turn the page and dive in!

– – – – – – – – –

¡Hola, chicos!

Soy Buddy, su amigo de Weekly Reader®. ¿Han estado alguna vez en un acuario? Estoy aquí para contarles lo que pasa en un acuario. Así que vengan conmigo. ¡Pasen la página y sumérjanse en la lectura!

Boldface words appear in the glossary.

– – – – – – – – –

Las palabras en **negrita** aparecen en el glosario.

Welcome to the **aquarium** (ah-KWAY-ree-uhm)! People visit an aquarium to see all kinds of water animals, from tiny fish to giant sharks.

— — — — — — — — —

¡Bienvenidos al **acuario**! La gente va a un acuario para ver animales acuáticos de todo tipo, desde diminutos peces hasta enormes tiburones.

The animals live in **exhibits**, or viewing areas. An exhibit is set up like the creature's home in the wild.

– – – – – – – – –

Los animales pueden verse en zonas de **exhibición**. Una exhibición muestra cómo sería el hogar del animal en la naturaleza.

Guides teach visitors about the animals. They help guests have hands-on fun at the **touch tanks**.

— — — — — — — — —

Los guías dan información sobre los animales. También ayudan a los visitantes a divertirse en los **estanques de contacto**.

touch tank/
estanque de contacto

9

Aquarists (ah-KWAH-rists) feed the fish and other creatures. What is on the menu for these sea otters?

– – – – – – – – –

Los **acuaristas** dan de comer a los peces y a los demás animales. ¿Qué habrá en el menú para estas nutrias marinas?

aquarist/
acuarista

Aquarists care for the exhibits, too. They dive in to clean the big exhibits. The divers wear **wet suits**. They use special masks to breathe underwater.

– – – – – – – – – –

Los acuaristas también se encargan de mantener las exhibiciones. Se sumergen para limpiar los grandes tanques. Los buzos usan **trajes isotérmicos** y máscaras especiales para respirar bajo el agua.

wet suit/
traje isotérmico

13

Aquarists check the water each day. They make sure it is not too hot or too cold for the animals.

– – – – – – – – – –

Los acuaristas revisan el agua a diario. Se aseguran de que no esté demasiado fría ni caliente para los animales.

What if a sea turtle gets sick? Animal doctors called **vets** will care for it. Vets do checkups and give medicine to animals.

– – – – – – – – – –

¿Qué pasa si una tortuga marina se enferma? Unos médicos de animales, llamados **veterinarios**, vienen a atenderla. Los veterinarios chequean a los animales y les dan medicinas.

vets/
veterinarios

17

Trainers teach beluga whales and other animals to follow commands. The animals learn to do tricks.

— — — — — — — — — —

Las adiestradoras enseñan a las ballenas beluga y a otros animales a seguir órdenes. Los animales aprenden a hacer trucos y acrobacias.

trainers/
adiestradoras

Workers do different jobs at the aquarium. They all have one thing in common, though. They love water animals!

--- --- --- --- --- --- --- --- ---

Los trabajadores de un acuario hacen distintas tareas. Pero todos tienen algo en común. ¡Aman a los animales acuáticos!

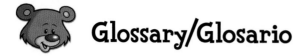

Glossary/Glosario

aquarists: workers who take daily care of fish and other water animals at aquariums

aquarium: a place where people can see and learn about animals that live in water

exhibits: areas in an aquarium where animals live and are seen by visitors

touch tanks: open-topped tanks where visitors can touch small water animals

vets: animal doctors; short for *veterinarians*

wet suits: close-fitting rubber suits that keep divers warm

— — — — — — — — —

acuario: lugar donde las personas pueden ver animales que viven en el agua y aprender cosas sobre ellos

acuaristas: trabajadores de un acuario que cuidan a diario de los peces y de los demás animales acuáticos

estanques de contacto: tanques abiertos en los que los visitantes pueden tocar animales acuáticos pequeños

exhibiciones: zonas de un acuario donde viven los animales y donde éstos pueden ser observados por los visitantes

trajes isotérmicos: trajes de goma ajustados que mantienen la temperatura del cuerpo de los buzos

veterinarios: médicos de los animales

For More Information/Más información

Books/Libros

Animals of the Ocean. Animal Show and Tell (series).
Kathleen Pohl (Gareth Stevens, 2008)

The Aquarium/El acuario. I Like to Visit/Me gusta visitar (series).
Jacqueline Laks Gorman (Gareth Stevens, 2005)

Web Sites/Páginas web

Georgia Aquarium: Kids Corner/
Acuario de Georgia: Rincón de los niños
www.georgiaaquarium.org/kidscorner
Visit the web site of the world's largest aquarium./
Visiten la página web del acuario más grande del mundo.

Monterey Bay Aquarium: E-Quarium/
Acuario de la bahía de Monterey: E-Quarium
www.montereybayaquarium.org/efc/cam_menu.asp
Watch creature cams, check out videos, and enjoy interactive
games./Miren las cámaras que muestran lo que pasa en el acuario,
vean los videos y diviértanse con los juegos interactivos.

Index/Índice

About the Author

Barbara Bakowski has worked in children's book and magazine publishing for more than 20 years. She lives in Stamford, Connecticut, with one husband, Chris; two children, Andrew and Amanda; and three dogs, Taffy, Trixie, and Tootsie.

Información sobre la autora

Barbara Bakowski ha trabajado en la publicación de libros y revistas infantiles por más de 20 años. Vive en Stamford, Connecticut, con un esposo, Chris; dos hijos, Andrew y Amanda; y tres perros, Taffy, Trixie y Tootsie.

24